Social Solutions

Written by: <u>Beau Norton</u>

CEO & Founder of
Health & Happiness Foundation

Go to <u>healthandhappinessfoundation.com</u>
for your free personal development tips
and tools.

My Experience With Social Anxiety

For most of my life, I was the "shy kid." I remember being fearful of social interactions ever since I was a small child. I couldn't tell you why, perhaps it had something to do with me being an only child who was raised by a single mother. Anyways, I suffered with my social anxiety all the way up until my early 20's. At 19 years old, when I was a freshman in college, it was worse than it had ever been. My roommate at the time decided to move into his own apartment for the second semester, leaving the room all to me. I was happy at first. I love my alone time. But without a familiar friend, I became more socially anxious than ever before. I was so scared to talk to people on my dormitory floor that I would only leave my room when absolutely necessary. I ate my meals alone. I studied alone. I did practically everything alone. During the first semester, I would drink alcohol about 3 nights a week just so I could relax and have a good time, however, it was having a major negative impact on my health so I decided to cut back. This made my social anxiety much worse, and I soon fell into a deep, dark depression that lasted many months. I'm writing this book to tell you how I overcame this immense personal struggle, with hopes that you can gain some insight into your own situation and perhaps follow a similar path for creating a better life.

To make a long story short, I did overcome my depression and social anxiety. Today I am happier than ever and have achieved some things that would have seemed impossible to the person I was just a few years ago. I'm still a normal person and I do experience some anxiety from time to time, but it is not anywhere near the level it once was. I am able to courageously overcome challenges and chase my dreams, and that is what I want for you. I know what it's like to live in fear. I know what it's like to feel worthless. I know what misery is, but I also know what can be done to steadily increase one's self-esteem and happiness. I turned years of suffering into a life of joy and satisfaction. You can too.

The following chapters will explain multiple strategies that you can use to overcome anxiety, depression, and low self-esteem. Each one is powerful and potentially life-changing. I learned these strategies from a handful of extremely successful people, and I've successfully used the strategies myself to overcome countless struggles and challenges. I would not even consider telling you about these methods if they did not help me personally. I encourage you to take these strategies and techniques seriously, because they will transform nearly every area of your life. The person you desire to become is certainly within reach. I want to help you make that dream a reality. Let's see what it's going to take, shall we?

Problem or Opportunity? The Importance of Self-Awareness and Solution-Oriented Thinking.

The first step towards positive change is *awareness*. If you are reading this, then congratulations, you have just taken an important step towards a better life. Some people will deny their problems and take them to the grave, but not you. You are different. You are honest with yourself, and you aren't afraid to seek for help. Now, it's time to really open up. It's time to be brutally honest and admit that you are sick of living in fear. I know you want to live abundantly and be courageous and confident. Don't we all? Fortunately, we all were born with infinite potential, and everything we desire can indeed become a reality. It's important to acknowledge the problem, but it's more important to focus on the *solution*.

When you are living a life that isn't aligned with your true desires, it is very easy to fall into the trap of pessimism and constant worry. This only serves one purpose: *to make you suffer so much that you have no choice but to change your ways!* I had to learn the hard way. I hit a point where the pain was so deep that I decided to dedicate my life to self-improvement. Perhaps you have already reached that point, but if not, I would rather see you avoid it. You can avoid any deeper suffering by choosing to focus on solutions rather than problems. In other words, you can consciously cultivate a positive attitude and turn yourself from a pessimist to an optimist. This is one of the most life-changing decisions you could possibly make, and yes, it is a *choice*!

There are two ways to look at every situation. As an example, let's look at two people living identical lives. The only difference between these two people is their attitudes. Person number 1, let's call him Dave, gets fired from his job that he didn't like very much in the first place. Even though he hated his job, losing it makes him panic. He becomes outraged and fearful of the future. What is he going to do now? How is he going to pay the bills? How is he going to find a new job in this horrible economy? Dave looks at everything negative about his situation, and so he suffers tremendously. Of course, things will get better, but he is too pessimistic to see that right away.

Person number 2, let's call him Gary, loses his job too, but he doesn't panic. He realizes that this is going to force him to take some action, but he sees that as a good thing. I mean, he didn't like his job to begin with, so this is the perfect opportunity to find one he actually enjoys. The economy might be bad, but Gary knows that he has plenty of skills that will allow him to get hired somewhere else. In fact, Gary believes he is worthy of a much higher salary, so he makes a conscious effort to apply for the hard-to-get positions. He goes out the very next day and starts putting in applications. He is optimistic, and it pays off. One manager who interviewed him found his optimistic attitude very fitting and decided to hire him on the spot. Gary now makes much more money and is much more satisfied with his life. Getting fired was a blessing, but only because he chose to see it that way.

So, what happened to Dave? Dave spent a few days complaining about his old boss and worrying about his situation, so he got a late start on putting in job applications. He eventually applied for some low-paying jobs because he believed that was all he could get in such a poor economy. He ended up settling for a position that paid him the same salary as his old job. He's still not satisfied, but hey, what can you expect when you get fired from a job in a poor economy?...

I hope this illustrates the importance of having a positive attitude and focusing on solutions rather than problems. This is just one example of how optimism can enhance your life, but the same applies to nearly every situation. I don't expect you to switch your mindset overnight. I know it takes times to change your attitude, but it should be a top priority of yours. Don't worry, I'm going to give you many techniques for steadily shifting your attitude to a more positive one while simultaneously increasing your motivation, energy, self-confidence, and productivity. But first, ponder this:

Your dominant thoughts and emotions will eventually become your reality. *Thoughts lead to actions, actions create habits, habits create character, and character determines your destiny*.

The simple yet profound solution to nearly all personal problems is *positive thinking*. The way you think determines the quality of your life.

People with social anxiety tend to suffer with very low self-esteem. Their thoughts cause fear rather than confidence. Having social anxiety does not mean that something is wrong with you, it means something is wrong with your *thoughts*. No, your thoughts are not *you*, so you can take some pressure off yourself and relax a little. Negative thoughts result primarily from a conditioned mind. You suffer from social anxiety because your brain has been trained to perceive reality in a certain way. Eliminating your anxiety can be as simple as reprogramming your mind through repetition of specific thoughts and emotions. I will discuss some techniques for doing this in the following chapter.

Before I go on, I want you to recognize that there are no quick fixes or magic pills to cure your social anxiety. Many of the techniques I will mention in this book will help tremendously, but you will be disappointed if you believe that doing them for a few weeks is going to cure you. I'm not interested in giving you false hopes and empty promises. I'm here to offer you *real* solutions! I'm going to tell you exactly what worked for me, but keep in mind that I have dedicated a considerable amount of time to my personal improvement. If you want to live a magnificent life, then you may want to consider doing the same.

In the following section, I will give you 3 powerful mental exercises that will help you gain more confidence and cultivate a positive attitude that will serve you for years to come.

4 Strategies for Creating a Positive Mental Attitude

"What you think today and tomorrow, the next month, the next year, will mold your life and determine your future. You're guided by your mind."
~Earl Nightingale

There are many ways to interpret reality. One person may look at the world and say it's a scary place, while another will look and say it's beautiful in every way. Which one of these people is correct? They both are! Why? Because your perception of reality is what is true for you. The world is neither scary nor beautiful, it is whatever you make it up to be *in your own mind!* This is good news for you. It means that your fear and insecurity are just your own unique way of looking at the world, and the way you look at the world can be changed quite easily! Here are 3 powerful strategies for changing the way you see things…

Written Thought-Restructuring: Turning Yourself Into an Optimist.

For you to function confidently in social situations, you will need to learn how to turn your fear into a more positive emotion. Any negative emotion can be turned into a positive one by simply perceiving it differently. Your perception determines your emotional reaction. For example, walking into a dark alley at night might make you afraid, but that is only because you perceive that there may be danger lurking. You react emotionally according to your perception. Even if no danger is actually present, you still react as if it were. In other words, it's all in your head! Looking at your social anxiety in a different way will allow you to turn your anxiety into excitement, or even calmness. You get to choose. Here's how you can become the master of your thoughts and emotions...

This simple writing exercise will only require about 10 minutes of your time each day. I suggest doing it right before you go to bed each night. What you learn from it will be absorbed by your mind while you are sleeping, and you will find yourself slowly but surely waking up each morning with a more optimistic outlook.

This is a free-writing exercise. All you need to do is record your thoughts in a journal of some sort. Spend 5 to 10 minutes writing whatever comes to your mind. No matter how crazy or negative the thought may be, just write it down. Do not edit or censor yourself. Write without stopping for about 5 minutes.

Once you are done, re-read everything you wrote. Pay attention to the types of thoughts you wrote down. Do they reflect a negative attitude? Are they hateful, self-defeating, or pessimistic in any way? It's perfectly okay if they are. We all have negative thoughts. Most of us just aren't totally aware of them. Writing your thoughts down on paper is an extremely effective method for becoming more aware of your thoughts. Once you are aware, you can begin to consciously shape your thoughts and change your overall attitude and personality. Without awareness, this cannot happen.

Even if you don't notice any negativity in what you have written, choose at least one sentence that you think might be able to be re-written to sound more optimistic. Re-write this sentence at the bottom of the page. Directly below it, write a new version of the sentence that sounds at least slightly more positive. Here is an example:

Original thought: "I really wish I could be more outgoing and confident around people. It's so hard to make friends with my social anxiety."

New thought: "My social anxiety may be holding me back, but I am grateful for the friends I do have. I will get better at making friends, I just need to be patient and seek out some solutions to my problem."

Do you see how the second sentence reflects a more optimistic outlook? It focuses on 2 things: *gratitude* and *positive expectation.* The first sentence focuses on the problem itself and doesn't address a possible solution. Although the thoughts are similar, the re-written thought is much more solution-oriented and thus more likely to evoke positive emotion and create some forward momentum. A simple change in the wording of your thoughts can make a HUGE difference in the quality of your life and greatly increase your chances for overcoming your challenges.

The more you do this writing exercise, the better you will get at turning the negative into positive. You may find yourself feeling socially anxious, but you will stop and think to yourself, "Wait, I can learn from this. I recognize my fearful thoughts, but I don't need to let them control me. Do I have a good reason to be afraid right now, or is my mind just playing tricks on me? I can choose to see this situation in a more positive light."

When you get really good at this, you will begin seeing every situation through a positive and optimistic lens. Fear won't dominate you any longer. You will be aware of it, because you have practiced recognizing your own potentially-destructive thoughts. That awareness is what allows you to *respond* rather than *react*. YOU will be in control, not your fear.

The solution to your social anxiety doesn't involve getting rid of fear. Fear is present in even the most confident people. The difference-maker is *how you interpret your fear*. You can choose to see it as something negative or as something that will help you learn and grow as a person. Fear will always be there to some degree, but when you create a more positive attitude for yourself, the fear takes on a totally different meaning and becomes much easier to face and overcome.

This simple 10 minute writing exercise will transform your life in ways you wouldn't believe. It will steadily shift your mindset to a more positive one, and you will find your self-esteem steadily rising. You will be more excited and hopeful for the future. You will believe in yourself and your ability to overcome your struggles. A positive attitude will do so much for you. I truly hope that you take advantage of this simple yet incredibly effective strategy for creating positive change in your life.

Autosuggestion: Programming Yourself For Confidence.

Definition: *the hypnotic or subconscious adoption of an idea that one has originated oneself, e.g. through repetition of verbal statements to oneself in order to change behavior.*

In Napoleon Hill's famous book, "Think and Grow Rich," the term *autosuggestion* is mentioned many times. In his extensive study of confident and successful people, he discovered that nearly every one of these people used some form of autosuggestion to influence their own personalities and behaviors. The most common application of the principle of autosuggestion is through the use of *affirmations*, which you've probably heard of before. Affirmations are positive statements that, when repeated to oneself over and over again, influence the subconscious mind and alter behavior. Let's explore exactly how this works.

Have you ever wondered why some people are confident and others are not? I certainly have. In fact, I've dedicated the last 4 years to answering this and other similar questions. The most basic answer I've come up with is this:

Confident people are confident for one or a combination of these 3 reasons:

- They have been told by teachers, friends, family, etc, that they are confident and capable people. Their self-esteem has been reinforced by the suggestions of *other people*.

- They have had experiences in their lives that have forced them to take courageous and determined action, and through this action their self-confidence naturally developed. In other words, they *acted* confident to *become* confident.

- They decided to be a confident person and applied the principle of autosuggestion, telling themselves over and over again the things that they wished to believe about themselves. Over time, this message was absorbed by their subconscious mind and accepted, leading to positive changes in personality and self-confidence.

I will discuss all three of these things in more detail throughout this book, but I would like to first focus on the use of autosuggestion because I feel it is the most practical and easily-applied method for creating positive change.

Think about the words you use to describe yourself, especially when faced with periods of fear and anxiety. Are you reinforcing your anxiety by repeating self-defeating thoughts? Are you hard on yourself? I certainly was when I suffered from severe social anxiety. I thought that I was the only person in the world who suffered with it. I thought that I would never make any friends. In my mind, I was a failure. But everything changed for me when I started to *forgive myself* and *affirm my strengths* rather than my weaknesses. The natural tendency is to focus on what is wrong rather than what can be done to make it right, but this is a destructive habit. Using autosuggestion, you can create a more optimistic attitude, and that attitude is what will allow you to finally move towards a solution rather than focusing constantly on the problem.

I was able to drastically reduce my anxiety over time by repeating thoughts that were matched with *who I wanted to become* rather than who I thought I was at the time. I thought of myself as the shy, quiet kid, but I knew that was not serving me. I decided that I wanted to start thinking of myself as a confident and outgoing person instead, and so I began to use affirmations religiously with the intention of reprogramming my mind. It worked, but I made some mistakes along the way that I think you should know about.

First of all, it's important to realize that it is not the words themselves that have the power to change you. It is the *emotional weight* that the words carry. It is the *meaning* behind the words. You can repeat to yourself "I am confident" all day long, but it will have almost no effect unless the words also make you FEEL confident. For this reason, it is important that you *act out* the affirmations that you speak to yourself. In other words, use your body, not just your mind. This creates *congruence,* which is essential for making permanent changes to your behavior and personality.

When thoughts and emotions are aligned, the mind is easily influenced. You brain can't be tricked too easily. If you say "I am confident" but don't actually feel confident while saying it, your brain knows you are fooling yourself. Only when you match the emotion with the thought does your mind accept the message and make it part of its natural programming. With repetition, you can create self-confidence that is natural and effortless.

It is thought that about 95% of what we do comes from our subconscious mind and happens on autopilot. Our personality and the way we think and behave is controlled almost entirely by the subconscious mind, meaning we don't have to consciously think about what we're doing. Truly confident people act that way without effort or thought. The same goes for shy people. We act how we have been programmed to act. If we wish to change how we act, we need to change our programming, and that can only happen by influencing the subconscious mind and changing its contents. Affirmations combined with strong emotion is one of the most effective ways to do just that.

Keys to effective use of affirmations:

- Word the statements in the present tense *as if they were already true*. Use phrases like "I am" rather than "I will." You want these statements to become true for you NOW, not sometime in the future, because the future never comes.

It is just a projection of your imagination.

- Use as much detail as possible when wording your affirmations. Detailed statements tend to evoke stronger emotion, and emotion is an important factor in making affirmations effective. For example, saying "I am a confident person who exercises self-control and steadily moves closer to my ultimate goal" is MUCH better than simply saying "I am confident."

- Get your *body* involved in the process. Strong emotion is the key to making affirmations work, and emotion is experienced in the *body*, NOT the mind. When speaking, reading, or listening to empowering affirmations, act out the words. Stand tall, put your shoulders back, jump up and down, pound your chest, raise your fists in the air, do whatever you have to do to generate a strong emotional response *in your body*. This is the secret. Without emotion, affirmations are useless.

That's basically all there is to it. It is certainly not complicated, but it is essential that you use affirmations correctly. Remember it is not the words that have the power to change you. It is the EMOTION! The words aren't even completely necessary. If you can simply generate a feeling of confidence within you, and you do that every single day as much as possible, you will become more confident and courageous by the day. I will discuss other methods for generating positive emotions later on that will speed up the process of change, but do not overlook the power of properly-used affirmations. Get started using them ASAP.

I wanted to make things as easy as possible for you, so I've created an mp3 audio track with 101 empowering affirmations spoken over a hypnosis audio track. These affirmations may not be perfectly suited to your goals and personality, but they should be able to get you started on the right path. You can download the audio at the following web address:

healthandhappinessfoundation.com/101-affirmations-for-success-audio

I recommend listening to this audio track in one of two ways:

- Listen while very relaxed. Take several deep breaths before listening. When your mind and body are relaxed, the conscious mind is not as involved in the listening process, which prevents possible resistance to the suggested thoughts. For example, while fully alert, your conscious mind may reject the thought of "I am confident" because it knows that you are not a confident person at the moment. While relaxed, however, your conscious mind takes a rest and your subconscious mind becomes more susceptible to programming. New beliefs can be created much quicker this way.

- OR listen while taking a brisk walk. This way, you can get more physically and emotionally involved with the suggested statements. You can more easily feel the feeling of success and confidence while actually moving your body. This is another great way to bypass the conscious mind and directly influence the subconscious mind where all your core beliefs lie. Those beliefs are more easily changed when the body and mind are linked through physical movement or the expression of emotion.

You should now have all the information and tools you need for using affirmations effectively. In the following section, I'm going to give you some simple yet often overlooked techniques for transforming yourself into a more confident and capable person. These are the exact techniques that have worked wonders for me. They will work for you as well if you take them to heart and apply the suggested methods.

Modeling Yourself After Greatness

Here is something you can't deny:
Many other people have transformed themselves from *nothing* to *something*. People have gone from poor to rich, from shy to confident, from fat to fit, from sick to healthy, and the list goes on and on. But how did they do it? Ahh, well that might be a question you want to ask yourself!

You see, the blueprint for change is already available to us. If we simply look at other people who have achieved what we ourselves wish to achieve, then we can gain a deep understanding of exactly what it will take to get where we want to be. If we are overweight and want to get fit, then we can easily find people who have already done exactly that and learn from their journey. We can learn about the mistakes they made so we can avoid making them ourselves. We can adopt the same habits and ways of thinking and behaving in order to get to a similar destination. Everyone is different, but the blueprint for achieving success in any area of life is basically the same: *do what has been proven to work!*

I have applied many techniques in my own life to become a more confident person, but the most helpful thing for me BY FAR has been my continuous study of people who have achieved high levels of success and confidence. I have read countless books, listened to hundreds of hours of audio programs, and watched thousands of hours of videos, all in an attempt to learn *how confident and successful people think and behave*. The specific techniques and strategies have helped tremendously, but not nearly as much as simply being able to *peek into the minds and lives* of extremely successful people. Over time, many of their beliefs have become my own by way of osmosis you could say, and so I am naturally growing into a more respectable, confident, and successful person. I am not trying to *be someone else*, I am simply trying to become the *best possible version of myself.* Studying "highly evolved" people has been invaluable to me. This is an approach you may also want to consider.

If you aren't already, I would encourage you to seek out a few role models and begin to study them. Read their books, watch their videos, meet them and talk to them if possible, and just try to get a deeper understanding of what their beliefs are. When you get to know some of their specific beliefs about themselves and the world, then you can consciously begin to create those same beliefs within yourself using methods such as autosuggestion (mentioned previously) or visualization (discussed in a later chapter). Theoretically, if you have the same exact beliefs as someone, you are going to behave very similarly. If you want to become a more confident person, you need to figure out the types of thoughts that confident people are thinking and model yourself after that.

To get you started on the right track, I highly recommend the book "6 Pillars of Self-Esteem" by Nathaniel Branden as well as "Psycho-Cybernetics" by Maxwell Maltz.

Visualization Techniques for Creating REAL Change.

You've already learned some powerful techniques for creating positive change in your life, but now I want to teach you something that is even *more* profound and life-changing.

Hopefully, you now clearly understand that our thoughts are essentially what shape us into who we are. Some thoughts are forced upon us by others, some are borrowed, and some are uniquely our own, but the truth remains that we become what we think about most of the time. The paranoid person is paranoid because they think *paranoid thoughts*. Likewise, the confident person is confident because they think confidently. BUT there is a little more to it that you do NOT want to overlook.

Here is where many people go wrong. Pay attention...

A thought is a mental picture. When I say ELEPHANT, what pops into your head? Probably an image of an elephant. Makes sense, but now what if I say the word SUCCESS? Chances are, the picture that popped into your head will be very different from the one that popped into someone else's. Why? Because humans are unique and interpret things differently. "Success" can have many meanings and can make people feel a wide variety of feelings, depending on the mental picture that results from the initial thought. For example, the word "success" might make one person think of luxurious vacations, fast cars, and crazy parties. That person feels *great* when thinking about success. However, the word "success" for a different person might bring up thoughts and feelings of resentment, unworthiness, and guilt. Or it might make one think of the *opposite* of success instead of success itself. Thinking of one thing often brings attention to the LACK of something else.

Why is this distinction important? Well, if you remember, I talked about how EMOTION was the major factor in determining how effective the use of affirmations would be. Well, that is true for any mindset-development strategy. Words don't have any power. It is the *meaning* behind the words and the *emotional response* to the words that is truly life-transforming. For this reason, you want to be careful when using affirmations. Choose the statements you repeat to yourself wisely. If something makes you FEEL bad, then it probably IS bad.

Don't get me wrong, affirmations are very powerful as long as they make you *feel good*. But I have discovered a much better technique that I believe should be used above all others, and that is *visualization*. You may have heard a lot about visualization before, but let me tell you a little about why it can be so powerful and life-changing.

Visualization, unlike affirmations, does not require the use of words. Like I mentioned, words can be interpreted in many different ways. Just because "success" is usually regarded as a "positive" term does not mean that it will be perceived that way by everyone. You may even *consciously* believe that "success" is a good thing but *unconsciously* believe the opposite. ALWAYS use your feelings as a guide rather than your logical thought process for determining the best use of visualization or affirmations. If a thought makes you FEEL good, that is how you know whether it is benefitting you or not. Visualization works so well because it allows you to skip the logical thinking and go directly to the world of emotions where all the REAL change happens.

In the following section, I will give you an extremely powerful visualization strategy for creating rapid positive change. You won't want to skip this one! If you only do one thing mentioned in this book, make it this one!

The Ideal You: A Powerful Visualization Exercise That Will Change Your Personality and Behavior.

For many years of my life, I was shy and insecure. For as long as I can remember, I had the habit of observing other people and comparing them to myself. I always wondered what made some people more confident and outgoing than others. I couldn't understand why some people found it so easy to make friends and express themselves. Was there something wrong with me? For a long time that is what I believed, until I realized that I had simply become who I imagined myself to be. I decided to imagine something different, and that is when the magic happened…

It is important to understand that everything we tell ourselves about who we are is just a made-up story in our heads. We are only limited by our own beliefs. Even the excuse of "It's in my genetics" is no longer valid. It has now been clearly proven that genetic expression can be changed by our thoughts, emotions, and the environment we find ourselves in (one good reason to surround yourself with positive people). We are entirely responsible for who we become. In order to take responsibility for who we become rather than being a leaf in the wind, we must choose to believe a different story about ourselves. That can only be done by *repeating a different story*, and stories are best told through movies…

What you will need to do for this powerful visualization exercise is create a new mental movie of your life. This movie needs to be detailed and vivid in your imagination. And most importantly, the movie must portray you as the confident, happy, successful person you desire to be. You must imagine yourself as someone greater before you will ever become greater. You must break the spell you've been under and stop thinking in terms of mediocrity, fear, and insecurity.

You must choose a new story for yourself. As you begin to replay that story over and over again in your own mind, you will begin to replay that same story in real life. This is what you've been doing unconsciously for years. But this time you will be the hero of your movie.

The change will be gradual, but things will be different. You are about to start taking control of your life and shaping yourself into who you desire to be rather than what you've been conditioned to believe. You are only defined by the way you define yourself.

This visualization exercise will require some paper and a pen to begin. Please do not neglect to do this. It is the single most important thing you could do for your future in my opinion. What you will be doing is creating a detailed description of your life, not as it is now, but as you wish it to be. There are no limits with this. Think BIG. What would your ideal life look like? How would you walk, talk, and behave in the world? What kind of friends would you have? What would you do for a living? Where would you live? Imagine this perfect future of yours in vivid detail. Take a few moments to imagine it in your mind, then you will need to work on creating a detailed, written description of it.

Before you go to sleep tonight, I want you to take at least 30 minutes to write out a detailed description of yourself and your life as if it were absolutely perfect. This is an opportunity for you to dream big and use your imagination. As you will soon see, this fantasy life you will be describing is MUCH more than that. *It is the blueprint for your future!* As you imagine, so you become.

Why are confident people confident? Because they've created the habit (unconsciously in most cases) of imagining themselves as confident people. You can do the same thing and become whoever you want to be! This works, trust me. I will explain the science behind it shortly.

The more detailed your written description, the better. Try to really immerse yourself in this fantasy world and feel what it would feel like. Describe the sensations, sights, thoughts, experiences, etc. Just make sure they are all positive. This is your future you are planning, so make it as bright as possible. No limits. Imagine yourself as the greatest version of yourself. Imagine yourself living a life free of anxiety and fear. Imagine yourself thriving in all aspects, and express that experience in writing. Do not write things like "I will have (this or that)." Instead, write it as if you already had everything you could possibly desire. Describe your ideal life as if you were already living it right now! You only need to do this once, but it is important that you do it right the first time.

I personally used 10 full pages to write out the description of my ideal life. You'll want to fill as many pages as possible. Longer doesn't mean better, but detail is very important. You will be using this written description to help you visualize. Just like an author uses detailed descriptions to paint a mental picture in the mind of the reader, you will be using this written description to paint the picture of your future in your mind.

I did this exercise over 2 years ago. Amazingly, much of what I wrote has come true for me. Back then, many of the things I wrote down seemed very farfetched. For example, I wrote down that I would be financially free and live in a house overlooking the ocean. Keep in mind that back then I was working a minimum wage job and was 20 thousand dollars in debt, with no idea how I would make any of this come true. Well, today I am financially independent, and next month I will be moving into a condo on the beach overlooking the ocean! I am truly living my dreams! I don't say this to brag, I am telling you this to let you know that whatever you desire can become your reality if you just do a few simple things and adjust the way you think. You don't need to know *how* you are going to do it. You just need to know *that you are going to do it!*

Once you complete your detailed description of your ideal life, you will be ready to start visualizing. To begin with, just simply re-read what you've written. Read it a minimum of 2 times each day. Before you go to bed and first thing in the morning are the best times because that is when your subconscious mind is most receptive to suggestion. Do this without fail for at least 2 weeks. However, if you really want to see amazing results with this, I suggest you do it indefinitely.

As you constantly re-read this description of your ideal life, the mental movie of it will become very clear and vivid in your imagination. As the movie becomes more detailed and clear in your mind, your emotional reaction to the mental movie will become stronger. Your level of belief in yourself will slowly rise. You will begin daydreaming about your future. You will find yourself desiring much bigger things for yourself. You will grow more and more tired of living in fear. This simple visualization exercise will change your life in incredible ways, and it will require little effort on your part. The mental movie you create for yourself will generate so much emotion within you that you will naturally take the action steps to make your vision a reality. You will move closer and closer to everything you desire, simply by painting the picture of it in your mind.

You will also notice your confidence rising and your behavior changing. When you visualize yourself as a confident person living your dreams, you will naturally start to think of yourself more highly. You will in time become the person you have imagined. This is not magic. Remember, this is what you've been doing your entire life. You just haven't been aware of it. Now is your chance to create your own destiny. The power is within you and it's up to you to use it wisely. This power does not know the difference between good and bad. Whatever you focus your attention on is what you will create. Make sure you are envisioning the very best future possible for you.

The Science Behind Visualization

Some people believe theories like the "law of attraction" are a bunch of woo woo nonsense, but many quantum physicists have already proven scientifically that we do in fact create reality with our thoughts. This is sometimes referred to as the "collapse of the wave function" in quantum physics. I won't bore you with all the details, but you may want to do some research for yourself just to reinforce this material. Right now, I just want to briefly describe the science behind visualization in more mechanical, easy-to-understand terms.

There is a part of your brain called the "reticular activating system" or RAS. All the information that comes into your brain is filtered through this part of the brain. It is responsible for choosing the information that is most relevant and useful to you and eliminating the irrelevant information. For example, if you own a blue ford pickup truck, your reticular activating system will cause you to notice other blue trucks on the road. It will filter out most of the other vehicles and they won't even cross your mind. Surely, you've experienced this before. This same phenomena occurs in every area of your life, although you may not be completely aware of it.

For most of my life, I was a pessimist. I would always look at the negative side of every situation. Many people accept that the world is a negative place, but is it really? *The world is actually whatever you make it up to be in your own mind. Things only seem negative when you have trained your reticular activating system to notice everything that's negative!* My negative attitude at the time was causing me to notice everything negative and ignore all the positive things about my life. I had to retrain my brain and make my reticular activating system work *for* me rather than *against* me. This is essentially what you will be doing using the methods and techniques in this book.

By visualizing your ideal future, you are basically programming your mind to start noticing all the things in your life that will help you to move towards your goal. If you continue focusing on your fears and worries, your reticular activating system will make you completely blind to the things that will help you get to where you actually want to go. It will instead cause you to notice all the things that bring you fear and worry. This is why it is so essential that you spend as much time as possible visualizing what you *want* rather than what you *don't want*. Whatever you focus on will gradually make its way into your reality by way of the reticular activating system.

When you consistently focus on the best possible outcomes, you will consistently find the people and resources you need to make those imagined outcomes a reality. If you don't look on the bright side of things, you will inevitably miss those opportunities.

The other major reason for the effectiveness of visualization is the connections that it forms in your brain. It is similar to the process that takes place when you create a new habit. When you do something over and over again, you form a stronger and stronger connection between the neurons in your brain, until eventually that behavior is automatic and totally natural. Visualizing yourself behaving in a certain way will actually strengthen the neuro-pathways in your brain associated with that behavior. This is especially true when you combine the thought with strong emotion. So if you want to behave more confidently in social situations, for example, you could simply visualize yourself doing so until that becomes your natural way of behaving. If you are committed, you can certainly reverse your social anxiety using this method.

Don't get me wrong, you will still need experience to become truly confident. What I'm talking about here is mostly what I like to call "ego confidence." The other half of the equation involves the body, which is exactly what I will be talking about in the following chapters. You now know everything you need to know to start reprogramming your mind. That alone will be the catalyst for great things to come. Now let me show you how you can dramatically speed up this whole personal transformation process.

Bioenergetics: Releasing Tension and Allowing Joyful Expression.

I've spoken a lot about the mind thus far, but now I want to talk about the *body*. The body is the expression of the mind and is directly affected by our thoughts. Likewise, the the mind is affected by the body. It goes both ways. Understanding the mind-body connection is key to alleviating stress, anxiety, depression, and other negative emotions. When you understand how this connection works, you can speed up the rate at which you overcome these things quite dramatically.

The mind-body connection is the primary reason all the strategies mentioned in this book work so well. As mentioned, when working directly with the mind, it is important to incorporate *emotion*. Emotion is the expression of the body. Thought is the expression of the mind. When combined, a powerfully transformative process begins. Remember though, the mind-body connection goes both ways. You can use this fact to your advantage.

Think of the mind-body connection as a perpetual loop. The thoughts you think cause the emotions you feel. These emotions then cause more thoughts, and the process continues for as long as you let it. Most people never become aware of this loop, and so the cycle continues on and on, often causing a whole slew of negative emotions, panic attacks, depression, etc. This cycle wouldn't be such a bad thing if it was a positive one, but that's usually not the case. Most people have negative thoughts that lead to negative emotions, which then reinforce the negative thoughts, and the downward spiral perpetuates. You'll want to do everything possible to reverse this cycle.

You have already learned how to fix the mental side of things, but that may take some time. You've probably created the habit of negative thinking over the years, and so negative thoughts will naturally surface as you go through the process of restructuring your overall attitude and perception. In order to speed up the process and eliminate your negative thoughts and emotions quickly, direct work with the body is necessary.

In my study of bioenergetics (reading the books of Alexander Lowen), I have come to understand that psychological issues often manifest themselves in the body and can become trapped there. Working with the mind only is not always effective because it is not a holistic approach to personal development. The mind and the body are not separate. The nervous system that extends through every inch of your body is connected directly to your brain. Therefore, what happens in your brain also happens in your body and vice versa.

Psychological stress manifests itself as physical stress. Negative thinking causes negative emotions. If those emotions are suppressed in any way, they become trapped in the musculature of your body and create physical tension and stress. This physical stress can then have a direct impact (negative usually) on your thinking process without you even realizing it.

You can reverse the thinking processes that causes the psychological stress in the first place, but that may not create permanent change due to the patterns of stress that have been created in the body (similar to a habit created in the mind). Therefore, we must work to eliminate not only the negative mental patterns but the negative physical patterns as well. Thanks to the science of bioenergetics, we can take simple steps to do just that.

I want to make this as simple as possible for you, so I'm just going to give you the basic information. What bioenergetics boils down to is the expression of unreleased energy. By releasing physical tension, we can simultaneously release psychological tension, thus reducing the chance that negative thoughts will continue to inhabit the mind. The mind is the body. Freeing the body of stress also frees the mind of stress and allows it to work much better. By integrating some of the following bioenergetic exercises with the mental exercises you learned previously, you will allow for rapid positive changes in your levels of happiness and your feelings of personal power.

It is well-known today that many people do not have the ability to experience the higher emotions such as joy and ecstasy simply because they have so much tension trapped in the musculature of their bodies. In order to experience positive emotions, the energy in the body needs to flow freely. Tension in the muscles prevents this from happening, and so many people live their entire lives only able to experience a small range of human emotions. We are all inhibited in some way or another, but our goal should be to free ourselves as much as possible. This will allow for greater self-expression, which leads to greater confidence, creativity, and overall fulfillment from life.

Self-expression is often the #1 obstacle for people suffering with social anxiety. This problem stems from the mind (usually a result of early childhood trauma) but is often suppressed, causing the energy to become trapped within the body and manifest itself as stress and anxiety. Thus the release of tension through bioenergetic exercises is of utmost importance to those who suffer with any kind of anxiety at all.

The following are some simple tips for expressing the trapped energy in your body. These techniques will slowly free you from the grip of fear and anxiety. The more you practice them, the greater will be your ability to express yourself freely. Speaking your mind will become easier. You will feel more confident. You will be able to experience higher states of consciousness like that of ecstasy and bliss. You will have more physical energy. The benefits are many.

1. Use intense exercise (e.g. sprints) or some other form of physical

movement such as dancing to release unexpressed emotional energy. This is the most basic way to release built up tension in the body. You can get similar benefits by using a <u>vibration plate</u> or getting regular massages. The latter are more passive ways of releasing trapped energy. These things all offer many physical, mental, and emotional benefits.

2. Do some form of "working in." This could be in the form of meditation, yoga, tai chi, chi gong, and many others. These practices are beneficial because they allow you to become aware of physical tension in the body. Once you cultivate awareness, the energy will begin to flow more easily and your anxiety will gradually lessen over time.

3. Practice radical honesty. Most people who suffer with shyness or social anxiety have a hard time expressing their thoughts. As I mentioned, these thoughts can become trapped as

emotional energy within the body and cause a lot of physical problems. Expressing your thoughts intellectually is just as essential as expressing your emotions physically. To learn more about radical honesty and how it can transform your life, I recommend the book "Radical Honesty" by Brad Blanton.

4. Be conscious of your eating habits. Food is a form of energy. It directly affects the physical, mental, and emotional energies within the body. Processed foods or extremely dense foods like bread and meat can cause energy blockages in the body, leading to stress, anxiety, and muscular tension. Eat more high-water foods like fruits and vegetables and your anxiety will be greatly reduced.

5. Do more of what you love and begin to let go of the expectations of other people. Most people spend their whole lives being someone they are not just so they can live up to other

people's expectations. This is very dangerous for many reasons. First of all, it prevents you from being happy and doing things you truly desire to do. It also results in *a lot* of suppressed thoughts and emotions, which often lead to physical ailments and disease later in life. It causes you massive amounts of unnecessary stress and drastically reduces the quality of your life. Start following your heart instead of your head, which is usually just a compilation of other people's thoughts about you anyway.

6. Do "The Bow" for 2 minutes daily. This is a simple bioenergetic exercise that releases trapped energy very effectively. Once you do it, you will know exactly what I mean when I say that all of us have great amounts of stored emotional energy and physical tension. This exercise is difficult to explain in words. Google the phrase "bioenergetic bow exercise" to see an actual demonstration.

These 6 methods are simple and extremely effective for reducing stress and anxiety. They are not quick-fixes but rather long-term strategies for creating positive change. I hope you consider putting them into action. You will be happy you did.

You should now have a good understanding of how the body and mind work together as one. You have the techniques for creating a new mental attitude, which will naturally lessen your physical experience of anxiety. You also have the techniques for directly releasing physical tension, which will gradually break up old thought patterns that are based on fear and no longer serving you. You have the holistic approach to developing yourself, now you just need to put it into action.

Environment and Experience: Avoiding Pitfalls and Accelerating the Change Process.

"The opposite of courage in our society is not cowardice, it's conformity."
~Rollo May

Everything you've learned thus far will act as the foundation for all the other decisions you make and actions you take on your journey of personal growth. As you create a more positive attitude for yourself, you will naturally make better decisions. As you release physical, mental, and emotional tension, you will naturally feel more confident and capable. But you *will* face many challenges on your journey. That is what growth is all about. In this chapter, I want to prepare you for some of these challenges. If you aren't aware of them, there is a high probability you will get sucked back into your old ways of thinking and behaving. This won't be a problem for you, however, because I'm going to address these potential issues in the following paragraphs.

Potential Pitfall #1 - An environment that is not aligned with who you wish to become.

This is important. If you follow the advice in this book but fail to adjust the rest of your life as needed, you will inevitably fall back into your old habits and ways of behaving. As you change your mindset using the techniques and strategies mentioned throughout this book, you will naturally begin to desire change in your outer world as well. But if you ignore this desire and fail to change, your old thought-patterns will take over. You must break free from the conditioning of not only your mind, but your environment as well.

As you change the way you think, people in your life will start looking at you differently. They may make comments about you "acting weird" or "not being yourself." Don't let these traps fool you. The people in your life have certain expectations of you based on the way you have behaved in the past. When you change your thinking and behavior, you break free of past conditioning. This will make some people uncomfortable. Most people don't want you to change. They may unconsciously feel betrayed when you change your ways. They may be resentful or jealous. They may feel bad about themselves when you make positive changes, and so they will likely try to convince you to revert back to your old ways. Don't listen.

You will probably lose friends, but this is a good thing! If you continue hanging out with the same people who have the same expectations of you, then you will continue to live up to those expectations and remain the same for your entire life. Although this is what happens to most people, it is not something you want to fall victim to.

The same goes for family. It is important that you remain extremely committed to your personal growth, because you won't initially have much support. If you do, then consider yourself lucky. If not, don't worry, because you will begin to attract the right people as you continue on your journey. When you become a better person, better people will notice and befriend you. You may have to travel alone for a short period of time. I did. But that is nothing to be afraid of. It is a great opportunity to get to know yourself better and discover who you really are under all the layers expectations others have placed upon you over the years.

The main thing you need to keep in mind is this: If you find yourself in an environment or with people that are not aligned with *who you wish to become*, then you're in the wrong place! Sure, these experiences can serve as valuable lessons, but it is far too easy to remain stagnant when everyone around you is living that way.

You need to shed your past and become the type of person you truly desire to be. That will involve changing your inner world as well as your outer world. They are connected just like the mind-body connection I spoke of earlier, and so when one changes, the other must change with it or else the system reverts back to its old programming. Think about it. A positive person cannot remain around negative people for long without eventually becoming like them. So, if you really want to change for the better, can you really afford to hang around people who are just remaining the same? That influence is too strong. You need to leave some people behind.

A total life transformation is often necessary. It won't be easy, but it *will* be worth it.

Potential Pitfall #2 - Staying in your head and not taking action to expand your comfort zone and gain necessary experience.

As I said before, when you change your attitude, your behavior will naturally change as well. When you start thinking more positively and confidently, you will begin taking action that is congruent with those thoughts. This is why the strategies in this book are geared more towards changing your "inner world" than anything else. As within, so without. As you think, so you become. This is true. But there is also a trap that many people fall into, and that is *living primarily in the fantasy world in your head* rather than taking action and facing your fears.

Fear and anxiety is present in even the most confident people. You will never get rid of it completely. You can affirm and visualize your desired result all day long every day, but what you visualize will not become a reality unless you take some action.

To be a massive action-taker, you need to develop the skill of present moment awareness. In other words, you need to get out of your head and experience reality as it truly is. Overanalyzing is the primary cause of fear and anxiety in social situations. To overcome fear and take the action necessary for personal improvement, you need to develop the skill of present moment awareness. When you are in the present moment (not analyzing at all), action happens naturally and effortlessly. If you just learn to stay out of your head in social situations, you will be much better off. So how do you do that?

The easiest way to get out of your head and thus out of your own way is to switch from *thinking* to *feeling*. When you experience anxiety or fear of any kind, analyzing the situation is the worst thing you could possibly do. It only makes things much worse, as you probably already know. The solution is to practice *feeling* your emotions rather than analyzing them logically. When you feel anxious, try to feel the area of your body where you are experiencing the anxiety. Feel the movement of the energy. Feel the sensations. Go within for a moment and really get in touch with your emotions. This takes practice, but it will help tremendously in the long run.

Even as you go throughout your day, practice feeling the sensations in your body. Start with your toes and work your way up to your head. If you focus your attention on a particular body part, you should feel a slight tingling sensation. If you practice enough, you will be able to develop full-body awareness, meaning you are able to feel your entire body at once. Most people never experience this because they are so caught up in their thoughts. But when you experience full-body awareness, your mind is completely silent in that moment. Fear and anxiety disappear in this state. If you can achieve this state of awareness while in social situations, you will be calm and at peace in your own skin. Conversation will flow naturally. No need to *think* about it. *Feel* your way through it.

There is another way to reach this state of present moment awareness, and that is by simply taking action despite our fear. This is a great way to quiet the mind and get into "feeling mode." When you are intently focused on taking a particular action, you are immersed in the present moment. Thoughts slows down, feeling takes over, and you tap into your true power.

Do the things you fear, and then fear will disappear. It works, but you have to discipline yourself to take the initial steps. It gets easier as you go, and I promise it will all be worth it.

Save "thinking mode" for when you don't have important stuff to do. When it's time to take action and chase after what you want, let your feelings guide you.

Remember, your own personal growth depends on your ability to expand your comfort zone. If you remain locked in your room all day, you might develop your mindset, but you will not have any reference experiences to reinforce those thoughts. Confidence is partly mental but it also depends on experience. It's like learning to swim. You can pump yourself up mentally to the point where you jump into the deep end, but then you have to actually put in the effort and learn to do the damn thing.

Proper Thought + Massive Action = Great Results

You need both parts of the equation. The action-taking is the hard part, but it's also the part that is required for reaping the fruits of your labor. Go make it happen!

Potential Pitfall #3 - Believing that the little things don't matter and avoiding the creation of positive habits.

If you don't start immediately and begin implementing the techniques you've learned in this book, then there's nothing anyone can do for you. You must take complete responsibility for where you are right now and begin taking baby steps towards your positive future. It is the tiny things you do on a daily basis that lead to major changes in the long run. This is the mindset you need to have.

We live in a "quick fix" culture. Everyone wants a magic pill. In fact, millions of dollars worth of "magic pills" are sold to desperate people around the world every year. Don't waste your money. The information given to you in this book just might be worth a million dollars to you in due time. I say that not because these strategies are groundbreaking in any way, but because *they work!* You can literally create any kind of life you desire if you take these strategies to heart and create the habit of using them on a daily basis. This is not just a book to help you cure your social anxiety. This is a book to help you live a better life in every way imaginable.

Don't overwhelm yourself, but start using at least one of these techniques today. Don't delay. Many people spend their whole lives waiting for the perfect moment to change. But that day never comes. The perfect moment is *right now*. Start where you stand, do what you can, and make a better future for yourself.

Conclusion: If I can do it, so can you.

Less than 4 years ago, I was at rock bottom. Today, I am more confident than I've ever been. My happiness is at an all-time high. Life is really working out for me. Am I just lucky? Absolutely not. I just made a decision that I was going to become the best possible version of myself and live a great life. I took the necessary steps, and I now reap the benefits of my persistence. The journey has been a bumpy one, but it's been so incredibly fulfilling. I promise you it's worth it.

Without the valleys, there could be no peaks. Each challenge is an opportunity to grow and become someone greater. But I don't want you to sit back and let challenges come to you. I want you to challenge yourself and take responsibility for your life. I want you to consciously create your own life as you desire it to be. You now have the tools to do that. You are capable of so much. Now go make your dreams come true!

Thank you so much for reading. If you want to learn more about me and access all my free material, you can check out my personal development blog at http://www.healthandhappinessfoundation.com

If you enjoyed this book, please leave a positive review on Amazon. Your support truly means so much to me.

Other resources:
Free Affirmations Audio Mp3:
healthandhappinessfoundation.com/101-affirmations-for-success-audio

My Youtube Channel:
BeauNorton.com

Made in the USA
Lexington, KY
18 March 2017